Aspects of Asperger's Syndrome

Success in the teens and twenties

Maude Brown and Alex Miller

P·CP
Paul Chapman
Publishing

Lucky Duck is more than a publishing house and training agency. George Robinson and Barbara Maines founded the company in the 1980s when they worked together as a head and as a psychologist, developing innovative strategies to support challenging students.

They have an international reputation for their work on bullying, self-esteem, emotional literacy and many other subjects of interest to the world of education.

George and Barbara have set up a regular news-spot on the website at http://www.luckyduck.co.uk/newsAndEvents/viewNewsItems and information about their training programmes can be found at www.insetdays.com

More details about Lucky Duck can be found at http://www.luckyduck.co.uk/

Visit the website for all our latest publications in our specialist topics

Emotional Literacy	Self-esteem
Bullying	Positive Behaviour Management
Circle Time	Anger Management
Asperger's Syndrome	Eating Disorders

ISBN: 1 904 315 12 7

Published by Lucky Duck
Paul Chapman Publishing
A SAGE Publications Company
1 Oliver's Yard
55 City Road
London EC1Y 1SP

SAGE Publications, Inc.
2455 Teller Road
Thousand Oaks, California 91320

SAGE Publications India Pvt Ltd
B-42, Panchsheel Enclave
Post Box 4109
New Delhi 110 017

Commissioning Editor: Barbara Maines
Editorial Team: Wendy Ogden, Mel Maines
Designer: Helen Weller

by the similarities to Alex's behaviour. She telephoned Alex's grandmother, Maude Brown, and suggested that it would be a good idea for Alex to be referred for a diagnosis. This was done and, six months later, after several visits to hospitals for various tests the diagnosis was confirmed.

Since her diagnosis she has mainly lived with her grandmother. Her mother is widowed, has a full-time job and looks after Alex's younger sister and brother. All the family live in Nailsea, near Bristol.

Like many people with Asperger's Syndrome one of Alex's main interests is the television programme *Star Trek*. The character with which she closely identifies is Data. Alex feels that the programmes help her to understand different types of people. Another useful programme which she enjoys is *Catchphrase*. This programme helps her to understand common sayings.

Because she has a good memory she enjoys trying to answer the questions on quiz shows such as *Who wants to be a Millionaire?* and she is very good at it. Her geographical knowledge often arises from her interest in stamp collecting. Another of her hobbies is cross-stitch embroidery. This requires a great deal of fine motor control and although Alex excels at it she has extreme difficulty in writing, and everyone else has extreme difficulty in reading it! Her college has helpfully let her borrow a laptop computer on which to prepare her work. This illustrates the contradictory nature of Asperger's Syndrome which often means that some skills can be easily managed in one situation but not in another.

Alex has very much enjoyed the local clubs set up for young people with Asperger's Syndrome and their families. They have provided her with friends who often share and understand her feelings. She now also goes to a 'Pub Club' where adults with Asperger's Syndrome meet for a drink and a chat. This group organise other social events such as trips out and weekends away.

Alex says, "Since I was ten I always knew there was something different about me. The other children would laugh at jokes but I could not see what was funny. I found it hard to make friends and was often told that I had no common sense. When I was sixteen and I got the diagnosis I felt an amazing sense of relief but I still expected people to misunderstand me. I didn't like telling people because I wanted them to see me, the person, not me the Asperger's. I see it as a challenge to be overcome and I like to help spread awareness and meet other people with Asperger's Syndrome."

Maude Brown was Senior Adviser for Primary Education in the County of Avon until her retirement in 1989. She was involved in the introduction of the High/Scope approach to early education in this country and some of the methods of working have influenced the strategies in this book, for example, the Plan-do-review sequence. Since Alex's diagnosis Maude's main occupation has been searching for ways to help Alex to overcome her specific difficulties but she has found very little practical help.

The best strategy that Alex and Maude have discovered for overcoming Alex's anxieties when she arrives home upset is to immediately sit down with pen and paper and write down all the things which are troubling her. These are written on the left-hand side of the paper and then they try to think of as many solutions as possible to each problem and these are written on the right-hand side. Alex is then able to refer to these notes whenever necessary. Sometimes it is also a good idea to analyse why the problem occurred so that it can be avoided in the future. They sometimes construct diagrams from the notes of their discussions and many of them are included in this book.

Caring for someone who has Asperger's Syndrome can be very stressful simply because they are frequently in a state of high anxiety. This makes it very difficult for them to control their behaviour. When she is calm Alex is a delight to be with, but when things are worrying her, life becomes turmoil. If she cannot sleep she will have to talk incessantly about her problems and this means that Maude has to stay awake for hours during the night and try to put things into perspective. It's a good job that she is retired and does not have to go to work the following day! From time to time medication to calm Alex down or to help her to sleep has been tried but doesn't seem to help. Many people with Asperger's Syndrome seem to react to medication in the opposite way to others. Families who have a member with Asperger's Syndrome will, from time to time, need support from Health and Social Services but this is very hard to find. Maude and Alex have had more help from voluntary organisations such as the National Autistic Society and Mencap than from the statutory services. Life is stressful enough without having to fight for every bit of help. However, things are improving and the Education services are now providing better support for disabled students. People with Asperger's Syndrome can be valuable contributors to society if they are given support when they need it.

This book is the outcome of the combined efforts of Alex and Maude. They hope that it may be useful to others who are seeking help.

Contents

About the authors 4

Introduction 8

Section1: Introducing

  Asperger's Syndrome 11

  What is Asperger's Syndrome? .11

  Circles of support 11

  Strategies for social situations .13

  Strategies to deal with rigidity .14

  Strategies for communication . .15

  Strategies to deal with sensory/

    motor difficulties 16

  Informing other people 17

  Asperger's Syndrome

    information sheet 19

  Rules 20

  Alex's rules 21

  What rules can do 22

  Decision-making 23

  Alternatives 24

  Problem-solving 27

Section 2: Daily Living Skills .29

  Organising space 30

  The daily programme 33

  Eating and drinking 34

  Personal hygiene 38

  Routines 40

  Packing for a holiday 42

  Shopping 43

  Managing money 45

Section 3: Coping in College .49

  Behaviour in college 49

  Punctuality 50

  Dealing with differences

    of opinion 50

  Questions 51

  Independent learning 52

  Assignments and planning 53

  Plan-do-review 55

  Progression in planning 56

  Study skills 57

  Developing control 59

  Developing a concept of time . .60

Section 4: Relationships 63

  Friends and acquaintances 64

  Dating .66

  Romantic relationships 67

  Valuing people 68

  Intimate relationships 70

  Allocating time to maintaining

    relationships 71

  Arguments 75

  Work experience 76

  Independence 77

Conclusion 79

Bibliography 80

Introduction

This book can be used in many different ways:

- by young adults with Asperger's Syndrome supported by a family member, carer or counsellor

- to provide patterns of organisation in daily living for those with Asperger's Syndrome and those who support them

- as a basis for constructing programmes of development for each unique individual

- as a discussion document for a self-help group of people with Asperger's Syndrome

- by a tutor leading a social skills course for people with Asperger's Syndrome

- as a framework for schools and colleges training their staff to understand some of the complexities of Asperger's Syndrome

- for raising awareness of Asperger's Syndrome among the general public, especially during 'Autism Awareness Week' each year

- by a Local Authority, as a starting point of courses for staff in Health and Social Services.

The aim of this book is to suggest specific activities and strategies to help overcome some of the difficulties that are encountered in everyday life.

Not all of the items will be needed by everyone, because we are all individuals with our own strengths. By using strategies like those in this book we are able to strengthen some of the skills which we may find difficult and which may not have been developed at the usual age. Practising these skills will help us to move forward to adulthood and independence with the confidence that we can tackle problems in an effective manner.

There are now several very helpful, practical books to help parents and professionals to work supportively with children who have Asperger's Syndrome. However, there is still a shortage of published materials with practical ideas for those who have received a late diagnosis. Alex did not know what was wrong until she was sixteen and the diagnosis came as something of a relief, but left us wondering what to do about it. We began to identify specific difficulties and then wrote down things which might help to overcome them. These could then be referred to when necessary and seeing them on the printed page made it easier to remember, whereas oral discussions were frequently forgotten.

Most of the diagrams, charts and activities in this book are those Alex found helpful and we have tried to suggest ways in which they might be adapted to help other individuals.

In some topics there are suggestions for activities which an individual could undertake alone, but it may be more beneficial to discuss them with someone in a supportive role. It can be even more beneficial to be able to do them in a group situation. In a social skills group each topic could be used as a starting point for a session.

Most of the book is written in a very personal style because it is the outcome of personal experiences. This means that it is full of examples which are not intended to be prescriptive, but which can be changed to suit the individual and can be disregarded if they are not needed.

We hope that the topics and activities will help each person to build up a personal pattern of skills which will provide a firm base of strategies to help make daily life easy and enjoyable. Most of us can tackle problems if we have a systematic approach which avoids high levels of anxiety.

One of the ideas central to the book is the Plan-do-review sequence (see Section 3). This was first used by the High/Scope Educational Research Foundation (1979) at their summer camps for teenagers from inner city areas. It was also used in schools for children with learning difficulties. They later adapted it for use by young children and it is now used in many schools in this country and also by Barnardo's in their establishments. Using this simple sequence can make life more productive and enjoyable for everyone.

Out of necessity this book is concerned with Alex's problems and difficulties but it has a powerful message to give: whatever the difficulties are, they can be overcome with support and persistence. It may not always be easy but progress can be continuous and can transform a life of bewilderment and anxiety into one of enjoyment and success.

Section 1 Introducing Asperger's Syndrome

What is Asperger's Syndrome?

If you ask several people with Asperger's Syndrome to tell you what it is, you are likely to get many different answers. This is because everyone is an individual and Asperger's Syndrome affects people in different ways. Similarly if you ask other family members how it affects their family life, you will hear of many different ways in which they manage to cope with potentially difficult situations.

However, there are common features which practitioners have identified. Asperger's Syndrome is generally viewed as a condition at the more able end of the autistic continuum and so the impairments of social interaction, communication and imagination are present as well as a narrow and repetitive range of activities. For some, the senses appear to give confusing signals and this creates a high level of anxiety. Some are quiet and withdrawn, but there are others who talk incessantly about their main interest. Asperger's Syndrome is sometimes called 'the invisible disability' because it is not always evident. People who have never heard of it will frequently think that it is just bad behaviour, and they will not know that the person affected does not realise that they are giving offence.

Asperger's Syndrome is not well known and diagnosis is difficult, so many people do not receive a diagnosis until they are in their teens or are well into adulthood. This means that they and their families have had to cope with very difficult situations, and in many cases the person affected has been blamed for the difficulties that arise because of their misunderstanding of social situations. This can have a catastrophic effect on their lives, making them more and more insecure and unhappy. This in turn leads to frustration, panic and outbursts of bad behaviour.

Once a diagnosis is received and accepted it is possible to minimise the difficulties if the person affected, their families, school, college or workplace colleagues work together with understanding and support.

Circles of support

If the diagnosis of Asperger's Syndrome is late and early intervention has not been possible it is even more important for carers and professionals to work as a team.

When Alex was nineteen she attended college to study Information Technology. She was able to cope well intellectually but found some social and organisational aspects quite difficult. We had acquired a copy of the book *Asperger's syndrome - practical strategies for the classroom* (1998) and found it helpful when used as a basis for a team approach by tutors and carers. The book has sections on social relationships, communication, imagination and rigidity, sensory and motor difficulties, emotional difficulties and work skills. Examples of how we used the sections on social situations, communication, rigidity and sensory and motor difficulties are on the following pages.

We used the book in the following manner:

- Alex was asked to underline all the items in the book which she felt applied to her.

- A two-column chart was produced with the headings 'Difficulty' and 'Things to try'.

- A meeting was arranged with her tutors and the first three charts were discussed.

- The charts were then used to help co-ordinate the support of both home and college.

- Meetings were arranged when necessary to assess the next action needed.

Alex was pleased that she was able to identify her own needs and appreciated the team co-operation for her benefit. Previously she often felt that everyone was 'getting at her' rather than helping her. We now plan to look at other publications to identify other suggested strategies for younger children, which can be adapted and applied to her age group and situation.

This plan of action may be useful for other teenagers and adults who are able to acknowledge and identify their own needs. In some cases, where the person does not want to know and is not willing to accept the diagnosis, it may be useful for the carer to underline the items they think will help.

The charts can then be used for reference and to remind the support team about strategies which may be effective. However, it is probable that most benefit will be found by those Asperger's people who have 'ownership' of the procedure and are fully involved in the chart development.

Strategies to help Alex with social situations	
Difficulty	**Things to try**
She is particularly vulnerable to teasing and bullying.	Raise awareness of difficulties and reinforce strategies for coping.
Alex can't tell when people are just joking. She finds it hard to know when tutors are really cross and when they are trying to give constructive criticism. She is reluctant to review and revise work because she does not see the need to do something twice.	Try to speak as calmly and clearly as possible. The raised voice, animated expressions and forceful gestures, which we tend to use instinctively, can get in the way of understanding. She may be alarmed by all this extra information and be distracted from the point you are really trying to get across. Don't rely on Alex 'reading between the lines'. You may need to explain exactly what you mean, particularly when it involves behaviour in social situations. It may be necessary to teach particular behaviours to deal with specific situations, e.g. how to behave when someone else is cross.
Alex gets cross and frustrated with other people. She sometimes cannot understand her own emotions and feelings.	Alex needs help to sense warning signs within herself and to anticipate problem situations. It may be helpful for her to have a 'script' or list of things to do when she is becoming upset or stressed. They may consist of either strategies to calm herself down or arrangements which allow her to remove herself from a situation. She may need to be prompted and encouraged to use these scripts and strategies. Continued...

Strategies to help Alex with social situations, continued

Difficulty	Things to try
Alex interrupts a great deal and has difficulty participating appropriately in group situations. She lacks the skills of commenting or building on the contribution of another speaker as a way of joining in the conversation.	Remind her that pauses in conversation are the place to come in with her comments. She may need practice recognising pauses. It may be necessary to devise an agreed signal used by supportive adults or peers.
Alex often appears rude to other people. She acts as though she is the person in charge, telling other people off. She often treats adults just like her peers and will demand an explanation if anyone (including tutors) 'breaks the rules' e.g. comes to lessons late.	Alex needs reminding about how her language affects other people. She needs to be made aware of respectful ways to speak to others. She should be helped to rehearse and try out a range of strategies.

Strategies to help Alex to deal with rigidity

Difficulty	Things to try
Explicit rules provide useful boundaries and guidance for people with Asperger's Syndrome, but they may not appreciate that there are times and situations where rules can be bent, re-negotiated or broken. If rules change or appear flexible, Alex becomes anxious and may reprimand others.	Think carefully about how rules are worded, building some flexibility into them. Explain why people sometimes bend or break rules e.g. a car exceeding the speed limit temporarily to move out of danger.
Alex can be upset by the uncertainty if routines are changed. Unexpected events can cause some problems. Some major changes can be accepted while smaller scale changes can be a real problem.	Try to give plenty of warning about changes and the reasons for them. Talk through what will happen and how she will be affected by the changes.

Strategies to help Alex to deal with communication

Difficulty	Things to try
Alex takes language literally. She has difficulty understanding jokes, sarcasm, non-verbal signals, idioms, metaphors and rhetorical questions.	Check back on what you say and re-phrase if necessary. Emphasise what you want rather than what you don't want e.g. "Please be quiet" as opposed to "I don't want all this noise, thank you."
The non-verbal communication skills we use every day may need to be specifically learned by those with Asperger's Syndrome.	For use by schools and colleges: use the checklist and teaching suggestions from the *Social Use of Language Programme* (Rinaldi, 2001) to work on specific skills. Encourage and emphasise her verbal strengths.
Alex has little understanding of what other people are thinking or feeling and so does not understand that her behaviour may embarrass someone she is with. Alex does not recognise embarrassment in other people. She does not recognise that her social behaviour is out of place and inappropriate.	Use a cue, such as a gesture, to let her know when she is talking too loudly.
Alex finds it difficult to cope with changes in routine.	Her written timetable is very important to her. It is helpful to have prior warning of any temporary changes and to have them written down so that she can refer to them if she should become agitated.
Talking about an obsessional interest without regard for the listener's interest is a common feature of people with Asperger's Syndrome. This sort of obsession may serve the function of reducing anxiety.	Use a 'code word' or agreed signal so that everyone can tell her when they have had enough.

Strategies to help Alex to deal with sensory/motor difficulties	
Difficulty	**Things to try**
Alex can be over-sensitive to noise. This appears to be linked to sensitivity to certain types of light. Extremes seem to be most difficult e.g. loud noise and very quiet situations.	Make sure that Alex wears her spectacles if light or sound is a problem. Background music seems to help her concentration.
Alex has trouble with some fine motor skills. Writing is a problem as she tires easily and it is painful.	The provision of a laptop computer for making notes in the classroom is helpful or having someone to make notes for her during lectures or lessons.
Words on blackboards and overhead projectors can appear to merge together.	The provision of paper copies of overhead transparencies is very helpful.
Reversed images such as white letters on a black background are difficult for her, as well as black letters on a yellow background.	Handouts printed on yellow paper are impossible for her to read. Printing black on white is much better.
For example, she has great difficulty in reading the number of a Bristol bus approaching at speed (a black number on a yellow background). When there is a line of buses, she misses the ones at the back because she can't see the numbers.	She could ask for help in the bus queue.

Informing other people

When Alex was at secondary school she suffered a lot because she was bullied. This seems to be a common problem for young people with Asperger's Syndrome. At that time we did not know that Alex had Asperger's Syndrome so apart from complaining to the teachers there was nothing we could do.

Alex's diagnosis came just before she started at college and she decided that she did not want the students in her group to know that she had a disability. Things did not go smoothly. She did not seem to 'fit in' and had no special friend in her group. She found it very difficult to join in with group work.

She struggled with the first year and so had to repeat it. On this occasion she decided that it would be best to tell the students in her group about her difficulties right at the beginning of the academic year so we produced the information sheet on page 19. Her tutor gave out the sheet to the students on Alex's course and answered any questions they wished to ask. Perhaps if people know in advance about difficulties others have, it might help them to be more tolerant.

This time things went much better and Alex now looks upon Asperger's Syndrome as a challenge to be overcome rather than a disability that has to be suffered. She is much more confident and has even been able to organise and lead some group work.

Activity

Everybody's situation and feelings are different. It may help you to discuss the advantages and disadvantages of informing other people about Asperger's Syndrome.

1. You will need:

   one person, with whom you feel comfortable (or a small group), so that you can share ideas

   paper and pen for each person to make notes of the points that you want to remember

   the information sheet on page 19.

2. Question to think about or discuss:

   Are there some situations where it is best to tell people that you have Asperger's Syndrome and other times when it is best not to tell?

3. Action for the group to take:

   Alter the information sheet to suit your own situation.

   Will one version suit everyone or do you each need a different one?

4. What is your personal decision about this?

   What other things might you consider?

   Have you considered the opinions and ideas suggested by other people?

Asperger's Syndrome Information Sheet

Asperger's Syndrome is the name generally given to people on the Autistic Spectrum who have average or above average intelligence.

Autistic people find it hard to:
- make sense of some of the things they see, hear, feel and smell because their senses seem to work in a different manner
- deal with changes to their normal routine, such as changes in the timetable or the room where particular activities normally take place
- understand some types of humour
- guess how other people may be feeling
- guess how other people might react to what they say
- take turns in conversation.

They take language literally and find metaphors hard to understand. When they try to understand something and cannot do so, this makes them panic. 'Perhaps' and 'maybe' are words they find almost impossible to deal with because uncertainty is very frightening. Things are either right or wrong and there is nothing in-between. It is difficult for them to see that something may be right in one situation but wrong in another. Once they understand a 'rule' or 'the law' they will obey it and expect everyone else to do the same. Even if they are very intelligent they appear to lack what most people would call 'common sense'.

Because of their literal use of language it is:
- particularly difficult for them to work as part of a team
- easy for them to misunderstand what people say
- easy for other people to misunderstand them
- necessary for them to ask a lot of questions
- difficult for them to understand unspoken gestures and body language.

What can you do to help? The following are some suggestions that may help:
- Try to be patient.
- Set ground rules before beginning group work. Make sure that everyone knows exactly who is responsible for each thing and write this down.
- If there is a deadline to meet, work out a sensible sequence and write down the date and time each item is to be ready, where it is to be taken and to whom it is to be given.
- Decide how differences of opinion will be resolved, for example, by seeking independent advice or by a group vote.
- If there is a personal difference of opinion during normal social interaction, say something like, "Let's think about it and try to make a decision tomorrow." In the end it may be that you both agree to keep to your own opinion. Life would be very boring if we all thought the same!
- If a task is not understood and you think that you may be able to help, please do so.

Rules

Rules are determined by society or a community in order to control the behaviour of its members so that frequent conflict can be avoided.

Examples

- The efficient organisation of associations such as the Football Association is supported by the willing recognition of its rules by all its members.
- The government of a country decides on the rules for its people. These rules become laws.
- When we play games (board, card or team games) everyone needs to play by the same set of rules so that arguments are avoided. If someone breaks the rules they are often accused of cheating and people usually avoid playing with them unless they agree to accept the rules.

Disagreements

When people disagree about how a rule is interpreted there is usually a set method to decide the outcome, for example:

- There is a referee for a football match.
- There is a judge in a court of law for the rules of government.
- There is a set of written rules for a game (or the rules are agreed orally before the game begins).

This use of rules helps us to avoid arguments and aggressive behaviour and helps society to function without too many problems. Rules are the basis of what we call civilised behaviour.

It can be very difficult to judge when a rule should be altered or ignored. We sometimes say that rules 'are not carved in stone'. This means that sometimes there has to be an exception to the rule or that the rule needs changing to make it more effective. You have to decide what you think is right. Sometimes it is good to get the advice of someone you can rely on. We can make ourselves respect the law and the rules but we do not have to expect everyone to do as we do. We are all responsible for our own actions. This is the responsibility that goes with independence.

Alex's rules

The following rules were written for Alex during her first weeks in college when she was sixteen. Rules need to be revised from time to time to suit changing circumstances.

At College

1. Attend all classes regularly.

2. In social situations do not talk about health, money or intimate family events.

These topics can be discussed at home with Gran, or with the doctor or your counsellor or your support worker.

3. Show respect for your tutors by listening without contradicting or arguing.

4. Model your behaviour on that of hardworking students so that you do not attract unwelcome attention.

At work

5. Listen carefully to instructions. Ask for help if you do not understand. Always do what is asked unless you think it is against the law or morally wrong.

6. Use a quiet voice so that people who are working will not be disturbed.

7. Notice how other people behave and try to do the same.

General

8. Keep to the agreed budget. If it needs to be temporarily amended discuss it with Gran first.

9. Have a shower every day and follow the flow diagram. Don't forget to use deodorant and to clean your teeth. (See page 39).

10. Leave the bathroom neat and tidy.

11. Always hang your clothes up in the wardrobe or put underwear in drawers or on shelves.

This agreement can be revised from time to time as necessary in order to accommodate changing circumstances and avoid problems.

What rules can do	
Positive aspects	**Negative aspects**
They help to organise societies such as countries, local communities, clubs, schools, colleges, universities.	If the rules are not working effectively they have to be amended by the group that originally set them up.
They help us feel safe.	If some people break the rules we feel insecure and someone in authority has to deal with the situation.
They help us to know what to do in certain situations. This can often save us a lot of time trying to make decisions and help us to make the right decisions.	If we have a problem and there are no rules for dealing with it, we have to guess or try to find a solution by trial and error. This can take a lot of time and sometimes it can be worrying if we do not know whether our guess will work.
Many rules are the outcome of experience of what works.	Sometimes what works very well for one person does not work well for another, so we have to make our own set of personal rules which help us. We have to make our own rules fit in with the rules of society.

Activity

Talking about rules and why we need them.

1. You will need:

    one person with whom you feel comfortable (or if you are a member of a group, work with a partner) so that you can share ideas

    paper and pen for each person to make notes of the points that you want to remember

    the list of Alex's rules on page 21 so that you can refer to it if necessary.

2. Question to think about or discuss:

   What rules can we think of which would help me in my school, college or workplace?

To start with it may help to identify things that cause difficulties and then try to make up a rule to avoid the difficulty happening again.

When you have written a list for you, write one for your partner.

3. Action for the group to take:

   Compare your lists. Which rules are common to more than one list? What is your view about this?

Decision-making

Some people with Asperger's Syndrome find it difficult to make even simple choices, but if they are given the words to use and are shown some alternatives they will in time begin to do so. From this simple beginning they can progress towards making more complex decisions. If the organisation of space, resources and time is well planned it will make it possible for them to assume control over some of their activities. Many stick rigidly to set routines because they feel more in control of the situation, but over a period of time they can be helped to be more confident and more flexible. For some this may be a first step towards self-discipline. It is important that 'choice' should gradually lead to 'decision-making'.

Choice is a selection made from a number of things. It indicates a person's preferences. Choices are frequently determined by the resources available and it may initially be helpful to limit the number of possibilities and gradually increase the options over a long period of time.

Decision-making involves making choices in a purposeful manner and is a result arrived at after thoughtful consideration. Complex decisions will involve numerous choices as well as the exercise of power. Both decision-making and choice play an important part in planning. We need to be aware of progression in making choices and decisions in order to develop planning skills, independence, self-discipline and commitment to learning.

Most adults automatically make numerous decisions every day without giving a thought to how complex they are. If we analyse what is entailed it helps towards understanding how difficult it can be for someone who feels insecure or who lacks confidence in their own ability.

Decisions that have to be made for practical activities include choices of:

- what to do
- where to work
- what to use
- how to use it.

Activity

Making decisions after considering the choices.

1. You will need:

   a partner to work with so that you can share ideas

   paper and pen for each person to make a diagram

   the diagram on page 39 so that you can refer to it if necessary.

2. Think about or discuss:

   Will a flow diagram help me to remember a daily routine that I find difficult?

3. Action for the group to take:

   Work in pairs. Choose a simple daily task that involves making decisions, for example, dressing to go out. (If you choose this you will need to consider the weather.)

   Draw a flow diagram to show the sequence of actions and the questions you need to think about. Remember to put the questions in diamond shaped boxes. How many decisions does your diagram involve?

   Try out the diagram before your next meeting. Can you improve it?

Alternatives

Some situations are more difficult to cope with than others. For most of us, making decisions can cause us to hesitate in order to think carefully so that we make the best decision possible. In order to decide what to do we may have to keep in mind several alternative actions. This means that there is uncertainty about what will happen and this can cause us to worry.

There are several things we can do in order to think things through clearly and systematically without becoming nervous:

- Write down clearly what the decision is about (the context).

- Underneath divide the paper into two columns.

- Above the first column, write 'If I do this...'

- Above the second column write 'then...'

- In the first column write down all the things that you can think of that you could do in this situation (if this is difficult ask someone you trust for help).

- in the second column write down what you think would be the result if you did each of these things.

If there are only two possibilities you should be able to choose the one you think is the best.

If there are more than two possibilities compare the first one with the second one and choose the best, then compare that one with the third possibility and choose the better of those two.

Continue in this way until you have reached the end of your list. Comparing two things is much easier than trying to consider a lot of possibilities at the same time. Also, if you work systematically through a list you will not overlook any of the possibilities. In the example on the next page some of the ideas may appeal to you more than others.

Alex decided to use more than one idea so that she could gain better control of the situation.

Context in which the decision needs to be made

My mobile phone bill is so high that I am very short of cash. I need to sort out how to reduce my future phone bills. Most of my calls are chatty calls to friends.

If I do this...	then...
Use landline if possible.	Calls will be cheaper
Use text messages instead of phoning.	This will be cheaper.
Restrict text messages to no more than 5 per day.	This will be even cheaper
Get a list of call charges and then phone at off peak times.	I can talk longer and/or save money.
Get a timer and restrict calls to two minutes.	This will reduce my bill.
Don't phone at all and do something else.	This will cost nothing!
Don't phone mobiles except in an emergency.	Phone my friend's landline instead
Keep a record of phone calls.	This will help me to see probable costs.
If connected to a friend's answer machine ask them to call back.	The friend will be paying for the call.

Problem-solving

When problems arise they can be solved in a similar fashion by looking at alternative solutions. A problem exists when what is happening does not match what you want to happen. We need to know what is causing the difference so that we can find a solution. Try the following approach to your next problem.

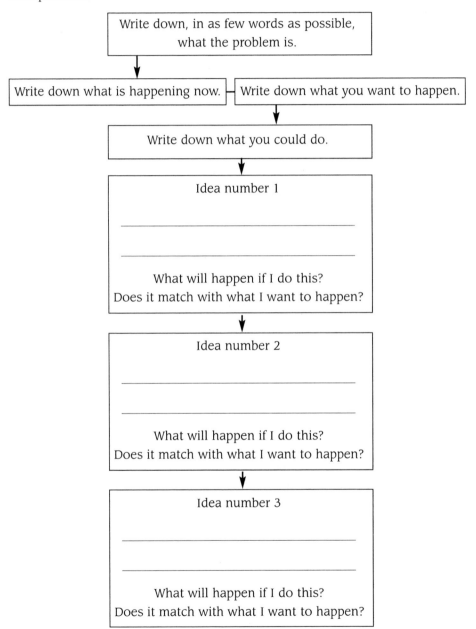

Go on listing ideas until one idea matches with what you want to happen. Sometimes you may find and use more than one solution.

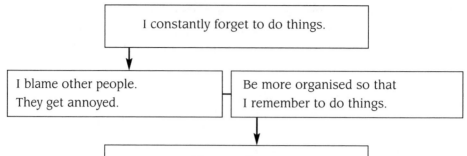

| I constantly forget to do things. |

| I blame other people. They get annoyed. | Be more organised so that I remember to do things. |

Idea number 1

Use a weekly planner.

This will help with getting to lessons on time. It also helps with timetable changes, and with catching buses by being on time.

It helps to write down changes or new situations as and when they happen, so that I remember to do them later.

I need to keep the planner, notebook or diary with me all the time.

Idea number 2

Obtain a handheld computer when I have enough money

This is slightly more reliable than Idea number 1. The information can be loaded on to a computer if necessary.

Idea number 3

Read *Time Management for busy people* (1998)
This will help me to organise time and be less stressed. I'll have more energy to spend on positive things such as coursework.

Section 2 Daily Living Skills

Many people find daily living very stressful but life can be made much easier if some aspects are efficiently organised. For example:

▶ Organising space so that everything has a proper place helps us to find things quickly when we need them.

▶ Organising time helps us to use our time efficiently, helps us to know where we should be at a particular time and stops us worrying about forgetting an appointment.

▶ Organising a budget for using our money will prevent the difficulties associated with going into debt.

▶ Organising shopping, cooking and sleeping can help to make sure that we have energy and stay healthy.

For those with Asperger's Syndrome, lack of organisation can be a cause of major stress and anxiety and as soon as they become anxious, organisational skills deteriorate still further. On the following pages we have written down the things which were of help to Alex. Some of them might help you. Before looking at Alex's pages take a little time to write a list of the things you have found helpful. If there are some situations you have not yet tackled then you could try the ideas we have written, but alter them to suit you. We all have our own preferences for things like food and the clothes we wear and so we will have our own ideas about the strategies we use in different situations.

Don't try to rush the process of adopting new ideas. It can take quite a time before you are comfortable with a particular sequence or strategy. For instance, it took Alex about two years before she could remember the full sequence for taking a bath or shower, so be patient with yourself.

Organising space

The efficient organisation of a person's own space can help a great deal in reducing stress. If a room is well organised it is easy to find whatever one needs quickly. The importance of the efficient organisation of equipment in the workplace has long been recognised as a crucial aspect of any business and it can be a great time-saver.

If you are lucky enough to have a room of your own, planning can be much easier. If you share with someone else then the organisation will need to be negotiated. The following ideas may help to start off your own organisation or alternatively could be starting points for discussion with the person who shares your room. Rooms vary greatly and everyone has their own favourite possessions so your own personal space will be important to you and very different from anyone else's.

Organising clothes

Clothes in drawers	Clothes on hangers in wardrobe
sweaters nightclothes underwear socks gloves scarves ties	coats jackets shirts and blouses trousers dresses dressing gown raincoat
1. Decide which drawer each article will go in. 2. Label the drawer to help you remember. 3. Use small 'post it' notes for a trial period. Make permanent labels later when you are sure that your organisation is right for you.	1. Hang clothes for school or work in one part of the wardrobe. 2. Hang leisure clothes in another part. 3. Shoes can be stored in the bottom of the wardrobe.

Interests and hobbies

Alex's list includes:

▸ cross-stitch embroidery

▸ *Star Trek* videos and magazines

▸ stamp collecting.

Decide where you will keep the things connected with each interest.
For example:

▸ *Star Trek* magazines in files on shelf

▸ stamp collection in stamp albums on shelf in cupboard number 1

▸ cross-stitch embroidery in drawers in cupboard number 2.

Work and study

Decide where you will keep things for work, college or school. For example:

▸ College or school books can be kept on a shelf or in a rucksack. Work things can be kept in a tray or on a worktop so that you can put them in your pocket or bag before you go out in the morning.

Planning the arrangements on surfaces

▸ Decide where large articles will go, for example, computer, television, hi-fi system: near electric sockets. It may be helpful to have the television on a wall bracket, which swivels. This saves surface space and allows the television to be angled towards different parts of the room at different times.

▸ Place the things that you use with each article nearby. For example, CDs and computer books near the computer, video-tapes near the television and video recorder.

▸ Consider using small plastic trays to organise small items. These can be kept in a cupboard or drawer and brought out when needed.

▸ Another option is to use storage items, such as a vegetable trolley, which can be wheeled into place when the contents are needed.

Plans for keeping items where you can find them

Alex often has difficulty finding all of the things she needs each morning before she goes to college. It is usually things that she uses both at home and in college such as spectacles, pens and pencils. It can be very helpful to have a special place for these things so that you know exactly where to find them. For example, if you have a 'map' to show where everything belongs it is very obvious if something is not there. Below is a simple map (or base plan), which is placed on the top of Alex's bedside table to show where to put the things she needs in bed each evening. In the morning she knows where to find her spectacles.

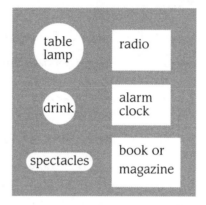

Plan for articles in daily use

The second diagram shows a plan for the things that Alex needs to take with her each day. It is a useful check to make sure that she does not forget anything. This plan can be placed on a flat surface and all the things placed on top of their outline. It will be obvious if anything is missing.

The plan could be drawn on the back of some spare wallpaper. If you like, when you have tried it out and are satisfied that it is how you want it, you could draw it on a piece of fabric which can be rolled up and stored in a drawer when not in use.

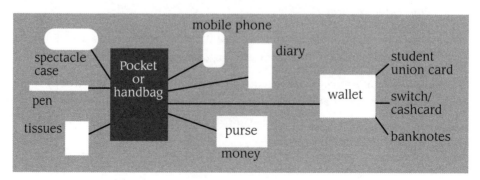

Useful things to help with storage organisation

- ▸ Hangers that hold several shirts or trousers.
- ▸ Plastic pockets, which fit on a hanger, for small articles such as socks, gloves, scarves.
- ▸ Plastic drawer dividers to help organise small articles in drawers.

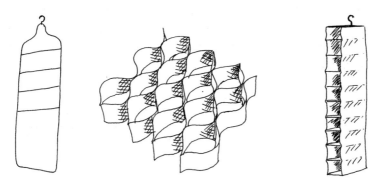

Articles to go on shelves:

- ▸ school/college bags
- ▸ radio/CD-player
- ▸ hats
- ▸ CDs
- ▸ books
- ▸ handbags
- ▸ bum bags

The daily programme

Time is a very elusive thing, which appears to vary according to what we are doing. When we are engrossed in something, time seems to go very quickly, but when the task we are doing is not satisfying or enjoyable it seems to pass very slowly. The measurement of time, like the measurement of other rather abstract ideas such as distance and value (money), is an arbitrary system employed by human society to help us make comparisons in daily life. Time is, of necessity, based upon the natural rhythms of our world such as the time taken for the world to orbit the sun and to rotate on its axis. All living things have a natural rhythm based on day and night and also on the longer cycles of months and the seasons. It is important to train the body to fit in with the natural rhythm of others in the community , for example, to be considerate and sleep at similar times to others in the family or in the wider community, to be active when shops are open, buses are running and so on.

Human society uses a variety of timetables but the majority of them conform to the natural patterns of our world. If we are at school, college or at work, most of the day will be organised for us but we are able to plan the rest of our time. As with most planning it is useful to make a list. Many people keep a 'to do' list to help them to remember what needs to be done each day. As each task is completed they cross it off the list. Whenever they realise that there is something else to be done they add it to the list. This list is an important item to help with their daily living and therefore they need to keep it in a safe place which is easily accessible at all times. A diary which will fit into a pocket or bag is a useful record. It can be helpful to sub-divide this list into three sections. First, all of the things we must do in order to function adequately; second, the things we ought to do; and third the things we want to do.

As far as possible things should be done in the order of A.B.C.

A. *Must* do	B. *Ought* to do	C. *Want* to do
1 Go to college	1 Start maths work	1 Hang out with friends
2 Hand in assignment	2 Sew button on shirt	2 Go swimming
3 Buy milk and bread	3	3 Go to the cinema
4 Buy toothpaste	4	4
5	5	5
6	6	6

Eating and drinking

When people have very good powers of concentration they often forget about time. They become engrossed in what they are doing, especially if they find it very enjoyable. This degree of concentration can be a great asset throughout life if it is sensibly managed.

Alex's main interests are stamp collecting, *Star Trek*, word puzzles and doing cross-stitch embroidery. If she is alone she will forget to eat and drink. It helped her a lot when her aunt explained how important it is to eat and drink regularly and to have a healthy diet. Alex asked lots of questions and the result of their conversation was written down in the form of a diagram (see pages 36 and 37). Alex finds it very useful to have things recorded on paper so that she can refer to them from time to time. She needs such prompts to help her to remember things that have been discussed.

Alex wrote down her own personal times in the margin to remind herself of the need to fit in with the daily programme at college. At home, in order to avoid arguments about coming for meals when *Star Trek* programmes were on television, the times of the evening meal were negotiated to fit in with the television schedules. If there was a reason why this was not convenient for other members of the family it was arranged to video the *Star Trek* programme so that it could be viewed later.

The results of such negotiations are usually best written down. It is sometimes a good idea to have a signed and dated agreement to avoid future misunderstandings. There are bound to be disagreements in any family and it is very helpful for people with Asperger's Syndrome to have written reminders. Sometimes it is also necessary for other members of the family! In a busy life it is easy to forget some things. In many ways people with Asperger's Syndrome have very exact recollections of events but at other times quite simple things are difficult to remember.

Activity

Planning the most convenient times for eating and drinking

1. You will need:

    one person with whom you feel comfortable (or a small group) so that you can share ideas

    paper and pen for each person to make notes of the points that you want to remember

    the diagrams on the next two pages.

2. Question to think about or discuss:

    What seems to be the most convenient time for me to have meals and snacks each day?

3. Action for the group to take:

    The diagram on the next page has a series of empty boxes on the left hand side. Think about your daily programmes and write your own times in the empty boxes. Compare each other's plans.

    If there are likely to be differences of opinion see if an agreement can be negotiated.

    Will you need different times for the weekend?

    Will you sometimes need a packed lunch?

Daily programme for eating

Meal	Example	Reasons
Breakfast: important first meal of the day	Porridge and fruit Egg and toast Bacon and tomatoes	Gives energy for the morning time activities. You should feel full enough to last until lunchtime (with a light snack about halfway between breakfast and lunch).
Light snack: sometimes this is called 'elevenses' even though it may be before or after eleven o'clock. It is so important that schools and colleges put it on the timetable.	Water is the most healthy drink but fruit juice without sugar can give you more energy. Many adults have a cup of tea and at biscuit at this time.	Your body has probably used up half the energy that your breakfast gave you. Your body needs liquid at this time.
Lunch: this meal is balanced with the evening meal. Some people have a cooked meal in the middle of the day and a lighter meal in the evening. Some people have a cooked meal at both times especially if they are using a lot of muscle power for manual work.	Soup and a sandwich or a two or three course cooked meal.	This meal gives you energy for the afternoon activities.

continued…

Daily programme for eating, continued		
Meal	**Example**	**Reasons**
Mid-afternoon break: this is similar to the light snack in the morning.Some schools and colleges don't have a break in the timetable because they finish at about four o'clock and students can have a snack and a rest then.	When people are at home in the afternoon they often have a cup of tea and a biscuit.	People need liquid half way through the afternoon. A warm drink can give comfort and warmth and helps people relax after a busy working day.
Evening meal: this meal is balanced with the meal at lunchtime.	Soup and a sandwich or a two or three course cooked meal.	People enjoy the chance to sit down with their family or on their own and eat a meal without rushing to the next activity. This meal is often a large one, to fill the body up so that there will be energy for the evening activities, especially physical activities.
Supper: this is usually a drink or a light snack before bedtime.	This may be a piece of fruit or toast or a biscuit with a drink. If people have been energetic during the evening they may have a sandwich.	Before going to sleep people often need to have a drink with a light snack so that their body does not feel empty and hungry but feels pleasantly full and comfortable.

Personal hygiene

Some necessary daily tasks are very much more complex than we think. It is remarkable that most people just seem to automatically absorb some procedures just by observing other people doing things. However, there are other skills which have to be learned, such as riding a bike or driving a car. Many daily activities consist of quite a long sequence of actions and these may need to be practised many times before they can be accomplished independently. One of the daily routines Alex found difficult was having a bath or shower. To help her we devised the flow diagram on the next page, which showed the sequence of actions and the decisions that had to be made at different points.

Alex kept a plastic covered copy in the bathroom and was able to refer to it when necessary. It took about two years before she could automatically remember what to do without looking at it. Now she is much quicker and much more flexible about whether she has her bath or shower in the morning or the evening. She also now leaves the bathroom neat and tidy for the next person who uses it.

If there is some difficulty for you in any personal management routine, you could try to work out the sequence of actions needed and keep a copy to refer to when necessary. It will give you a real sense of achievement to be able to do it independently and it reduces the amount of 'nagging' which parents have to do to get their teenage children to live amicably with the rest of the family. Perhaps most teenagers would benefit from some written prompts! It will also make you feel good when you realise just how complicated some everyday tasks are and how many decisions you will be able to manage independently if you have a visual diagram.

In this type of diagram the diamond boxes contain questions and indicate where a decision has to be made and the rectangular boxes give instructions. Other diagrams are useful for giving a sequence of instructions for doing straightforward tasks (see the diagram on page 41).

Taking a bath or shower

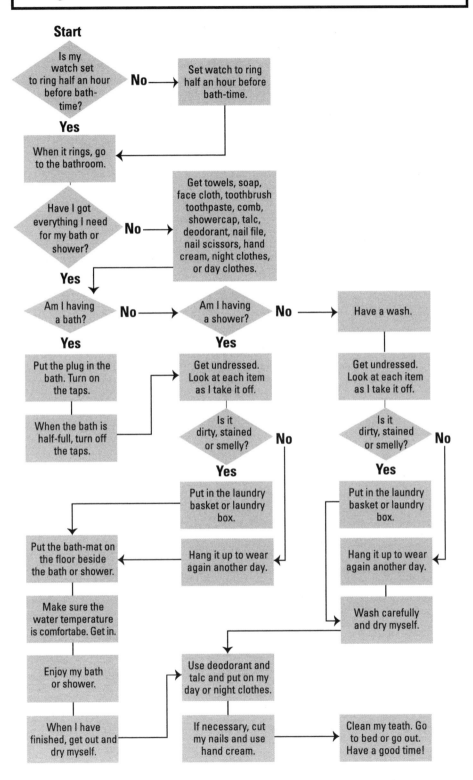

Routines

Routines are repeated patterns that help us all to anticipate what will happen next and thereby help us to make sense of the world. We are all familiar with regular time patterns occuring naturally, such as the different seasons of the year. There are other patterns, which we organise to help us with daily living, for example the pattern of the working week. Many people with Asperger's Syndrome have particular routines, which become inappropriately repeated over and over again. This constant repetition is associated with a high level of anxiety. If we know what is likely to happen next, this can reduce our stress and give us confidence to move on to something different, instead of getting stuck in the same repetitive action.

Many people today seem to suffer from stress. The explosion of knowledge and consequent quicker pace of change is one of the contributory causes. To build up confidence it is necessary to control the rate at which changes occur in our daily lives. For people with Asperger's Syndrome the pace of change may need to be carefully controlled in order to keep anxiety at an acceptable level.

Sometimes routines can be a real nuisance. If we feel that we must do something over and over again we end up being a slave to the routine and it makes life more difficult for us instead of being helpful. It wastes our time instead of saving it. We often repeat routines because we feel safe with something we know we can do. The difficulty in this situation is to bring the routine sequence to an end instead of continuing in an endless loop like the Sorcerer's Apprentice who cast a spell but did not know how to stop it! It can be helpful to write down the sequence in the form of a simple flow diagram with the start and finish items clearly marked. After the finish item think of things you may do next and write them along the bottom of the diagram. (See diagram on next page.)

From time to time, think of other things that you could do when you have finished washing your hands and add them to your diagram. You must wash your hands before some of the activities in the shaded boxes. Can you identify which ones? If you are lucky enough to be working with a group you can have some fun by thinking of some funny things to do and add them on. Perhaps you could all do a diagram of your own and then try them out and compare your results.

Sequence of actions for washing hands

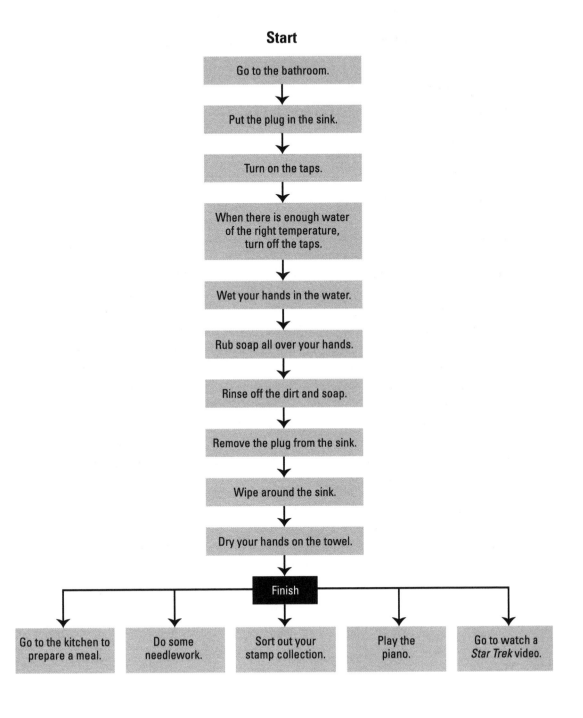

Start

Go to the bathroom.

↓

Put the plug in the sink.

↓

Turn on the taps.

↓

When there is enough water of the right temperature, turn off the taps.

↓

Wet your hands in the water.

↓

Rub soap all over your hands.

↓

Rinse off the dirt and soap.

↓

Remove the plug from the sink.

↓

Wipe around the sink.

↓

Dry your hands on the towel.

↓

Finish

Go to the kitchen to prepare a meal.

Do some needlework.

Sort out your stamp collection.

Play the piano.

Go to watch a *Star Trek* video.

When you are good at doing flow diagram sequences you may wish to try some of the following:

- instructions for making a cup of instant coffee
- instructions for making a cup of coffee using a coffee maker with a filter
- instructions for making a cup of tea.

Then when you are really good at it try:

- setting the table
- making breakfast
- cooking a meal.

Packing for a holiday

Sometimes changes in our daily routine can be fun but they can also be quite stressful. Packing for a holiday can be a chore if you cannot remember whether you have packed an item near the bottom of your case just as you have almost finished. You may then have to unpack and repack your clothes in order to find it. This is one of those situations where a simple list can be extremely helpful. Try using the list on the next page. You will probably find that there are other items which you will want to take with you, for example, if you are going fishing you will want to take suitable clothes and equipment so add them to your list. If you have a computer you could refine the list to suit your own requirements and just print your list each time you go away. As you pack each article enter it on your list and when you are packing to return home just cross it off.

If you are travelling abroad you will need your passport and details of travel insurance. A list of addresses and telephone numbers of people you may need to contact, as well as sufficient money (and your credit card if you have one, in case of emergencies) will also be needed.

Packing List		
Daywear	**Evening**	**Nightwear/ Underwear**
jeans/trousers shorts/sports shorts skirts T-shirts/blouses dresses/shirts sweaters/cardigans coats/jackets swimsuit	evening bag dresses suits	pyjamas nightdresses underpants vests/bras tights socks
Shoes	**Accessories**	**Toilet bag items**
walking shoes sandals wellies slippers evening shoes trainers	bum bags handbags scarves gloves jewellery camera/films	soap toothbrush, toothpaste facecloth suntan lotion talc deodorant razor tissues shampoo makeup medicines plasters

Shopping

Going shopping can be great if you are buying something connected with one of your main interests. Other shopping can be quite tedious and is best done quickly and efficiently.

Shopping for something which you are really interested in is usually very enjoyable. The main thing which Alex needed to watch was to keep a careful check on how much money she was spending on things such as *Star Trek* videos and stamp collecting. At present she has to be careful not to spend too much on telephone calls, especially to mobile phone numbers.

Shopping for clothes

Unlike many teenage girls Alex has never been very interested in fashion, so buying clothes has not been high on her list of things to do. We all need to think about our appearance. Unless we are in the habit of looking in the mirror every time we pass it we are often not aware of how we look. The way in which we present ourselves can have an important effect on how other people react towards us, especially if they are meeting us for the first time. Alex did not feel that she was very good at deciding which colours and styles go together. She needs help with choosing clothes for different occasions and so her cousin kindly goes with her whenever she goes shopping. Now shopping for clothes is not so daunting and Alex looks more 'with it', so this makes her more acceptable to her peers in college.

Think about the people of your own age whom you know well (perhaps someone in your family) and ask if they could sometimes help you to choose clothes for a special occasion. Clothes shopping is much more fun if you have company to give advice on suitable styles and colours and which are the best shops for you.

Household shopping

For household shopping which needs to be done once or twice each week it is best to have a reminder list similar to the list for packing. We found it useful to write the list in the order in which we walked around our local supermarket. Our headings for the list were:

- fruit and vegetables
- fish
- eggs
- rice
- fruit juice
- tinned goods
- breakfast cereals
- toiletries
- paper goods
- beer, wine and spirits
- meat
- dairy produce
- pasta
- tea and coffee
- biscuits and cake
- bread
- household cleaners
- sweets, chocolate, crisps etc.
- frozen foods
- magazines, TV guide, newspapers.

If you have a computer you could print out your list. Keep a copy on the fridge door using a magnet. You will be able to quickly make a note of the things you need, or if your list is detailed enough you will be able to tick them off when you discover that you need them.

Activity

Organising a shopping list

1. You will need:

   one person with whom you feel comfortable (or a small group) so that you can share ideas

   paper and pen for each person to make a list of the areas in your local supermarket

   the list on the previous page.

2. What to do:

   Think about your usual route around your local supermarket.

   Arrange the categories listed on the previous page in a sensible order for you to walk around the store. Compare your list with another person's list.

   Before your next meeting take your list and walk around the supermarket to check that you have written the list in a suitable order. Change it if necessary. Use it when you go shopping.

3. Action for the group to take:

   At your next meeting discuss any changes you made and say why you made them.

Managing money

Most things in life are learned gradually so it is important to start early. Although managing money can be complicated it can be taught to children in a very simple manner by giving them a set amount of pocket money each week and helping them to plan how to use it. Even if we have had the benefit of this gradual training it can still be quite daunting to receive your first income and to decide what to spend it on.

It is a good idea to plan carefully by making a list of all the things you have to spend money on each week and then put them in an order of priority. If you do not plan you might end up with an overdraft at the bank and this can be very expensive. At first Alex did not plan and because she was very interested in stamp collecting she wrote to a lot of advertisers and bought stamps by mail order using her cheque book. This caused her to go overdrawn and she had some high bank charges. However, she now plans very carefully and is able to save something each week so she has a reasonably healthy bank balance. As a result she has become interested in accountancy and has studied a short course at college. She now uses 'Microsoft Money' on her computer to keep a record of her spending. She enters all of the amounts once each week.

This is her expenditure list:

- food
- rent
- clothes
- fares/travel
- pocket money
- holidays
- miscellaneous
- savings.

Activity

Organising your budget.

1. You will need:

   one person with whom you feel comfortable (or a small group) so that you can share ideas

   paper and pen for each person to make notes of the points you want to remember

   the list above.

2. What to do:

   Using the list rearrange the headings to suit your own situation. Add more headings if necessary.

   Allocate an appropriate amount of money (weekly or monthly) to each category.

3. Action for the group to take:

   Discuss what each heading should cover. For example, will lunches be included in 'food' or 'pocket money'? Will Christmas and birthday presents be included in 'miscellaneous' or 'pocket money' or perhaps 'savings'?

If you are keen on computers you may have a spreadsheet programme which will help you to keep an accurate record. It is helpful to set aside a special time each week to review what you have spent your money on during the last seven days. If your money goes into your bank account once each month you may in addition need to spend a little more time at the end of each month to make sure that anything you pay monthly has been dealt with.

You may be happy just to have a simple current bank account to cater for all your needs, but if you have some substantial savings it may be best to get some advice about putting some of your money into a tax-free savings account where it could earn you interest.

It is very important to learn to manage your own money while you are still living at home so that if you leave home to live independently you will be able to manage all the household bills such as rent, gas, electricity, water and food, as well as your personal spending on fares and lunches.

Sample chart

Date:

Food	rent	clothes	fares	pocket money	holiday	savings	misc.
Totals								
+ or -								

A simple chart like the one above is a useful first time record for four weeks. It is rarely that we spend exactly the amount of money we have estimated for each item. Use the bottom set of boxes to record how much more or less you have spent of the money allocated to that heading. As time goes on you may want to add other headings or perhaps keep more details for some of the items listed. Experiment to find the system which suits you best.

Section 3 Coping in College

Behaviour in college		
College expectations	**Positive results if I do the things in column 1**	**Negative results if I do not do the things in column 1**
Attend classes.	People will think I am reliable. I will feel good.	Tutors and family will worry about me. Tutors will not be able to do their job of teaching and helping me.
Work hard.	People will think I am conscientious, I will feel satisfied with my studies.	Tutors and family will be concerned that I am not achieving my full potential.
Produce your work on time.	People will think I am productive. Other students may ask for my help.	Tutors and family will worry about me. They may feel I am not taking full responsibility for my work, and not asking for help when it is needed.
Co-operate with others.	People will think I am good to work with.	Tutors will be concerned if I disrupt the group and stop other students from working. People who disrupt other students' work are often asked to leave college.
Get a qualification and a good recommendation from college.	I am likely to get an interesting and rewarding job. I will feel happy.	I am unlikely to get a qualification and so will have less employment choices available to me. I may not earn enough money to pursue my interests.

Punctuality

Plan time carefully in order to avoid problems arising. Arriving late or handing in assignments late always puts you at a disadvantage.

Arrive two or three minutes early for lessons and appointments.

Complete assignments as soon as possible, revise them carefully and hand them in on the due date or if possible beforehand in case you are not at college on the due date.

If you are late:

Apologise quietly so that the interruption to the lesson is minimised. Give reason for lateness to the tutor after the lesson.

If work is late write a note of explanation and give it in instead of the assignment. State when you will be able to hand in the assignment.

If someone is late for an appointment with you:

Don't ask why, but wait to see if they offer an explanation.

If it is another student it may be possible to make a joke about it. ("Oh! I thought you had forgotten about us!") If it is a tutor it is best to say nothing as a joke may appear to be cheeky.

To avoid getting wound up about it try to think of reasons why the other person is late:

- ▸ Taxis, cars or buses may be delayed in traffic.
- ▸ Tutors may be delayed by an urgent phone call.
- ▸ Tutors may be delayed because they are dealing with a distressed student.
- ▸ The Head of Department or the Principal may need to see a tutor on an urgent matter.

Dealing with differences of opinion

If you disagree with someone try some of the following:

- ▸ Keep quiet and just shake your head.
- ▸ "You may be right but I think..."
- ▸ "I would prefer to do it this way... Is that OK with you?"

- "I'd like to consider your suggestion and discuss it with you later."

- Involve someone else to help with the discussion, such as another student, or if it is in class ask the support worker.

- If things are becoming aggressively argumentative make an excuse to leave the situation.

- Find further information to support your opinion, for example, in a text book.

- "I don't fully understand..."

- "There's more than one way to solve a problem. Perhaps we can think of other alternatives."

- If possible use "we could..." rather than "I want..." or "I think..."

- "Please will you explain why you think that?"

If rooms have been changed or lessons postponed use the following suggestions to help you:

- Go to the room the lesson is usually in.

- If the lesson needs computers, check in all of the rooms that have computers. Do this quietly so that any other lesson which may be in progress is not interrupted. If there is a window look through the window to see if the group is there. Otherwise open the door a few inches and peep in to see if the group is there.

- Write down room numbers on your timetable as soon as they are decided. Put temporary changes in the correct date in your diary.

- Always have your timetable and diary easily accessible.

- If in real difficulty find your support worker or your personal tutor. They may be able to find out where the group is.

- If a lesson is cancelled go to the library and study. Use the time profitably.

Questions

Questions are an essential tool for seeking knowledge. They are evidence of curiosity on the part of the questioner. In the learning process they can have both a negative and a positive effect.

In some situations questions can be very threatening, for example in a court of law. Sometimes we can feel very insecure when asked questions in an examination or in a classroom where our lack of knowledge may be exposed for all to see.

On the other hand, if we know the answer to the questions asked, our self-image can be reinforced in a positive manner and our motivation will be increased.

The most useful questions are probably the ones we ask ourselves. They are an important factor in making decisions throughout our daily lives and the effective use of self-questioning helps us in solving problems and completing tasks competently. It is possible that people with Asperger's Syndrome do not automatically use self-questioning as part of their thinking, so it is very important that they have help to develop this skill. (For some examples, see pages 53–56.)

At first Alex thought that it was silly to ask yourself questions, but doing this is a very helpful way to make yourself think clearly about many different situations. You don't usually say the questions out loud – just think them. It is also useful to ask yourself if someone you know would answer the question the same way that you have answered it or whether their opinion would be different. Comparing different answers to questions can help us to understand other people's points of view.

If we discuss questions in a small group it helps us to realise that there may be more than one suitable answer to some questions and that it is quite alright to have an opinion which differs from that of someone else.

When Alex was younger she thought that if someone had an opinion which was different to hers that they did not like her. She did not realise that people with very different views on something can still remain friends. It is our opinions about right and wrong actions which form our own individual moral code but we can still be tolerant of the views of other people.

Independent learning

In real life situations adults use a variety of skills to solve problems and to accomplish work efficiently. Most people ask themselves questions in their minds to help them to identify what they need to do, but many people with Asperger's Syndrome find this mental self-conversation very difficult. It may be helpful to practise using the following list of questions when you are faced with a particular task.

Adult tasks involve the following:

Questions asked in order to identify needs and strategies	Skills and knowledge used or developed
1. What will I do?	Identification of task.
2. What do I need?	Identification of materials and/or information.
3. How and where will I use it?	Identification of space needed. Consideration of aspects such as safety.
4. When do I need it?	Organisation of sequence of action and the use of time.
5. Where will I find it?	Knowledge of conventions of organisation used by society.
6. Where, or from whom, can I get help or advice?	Knowledge of retrieval systems and specialist knowledge which can be obtained from people.

Assignments and planning

It can be very daunting when you are first given an essay to write or an assignment to undertake. The two main problems are knowing where to start and what information to include. It helps a lot if you have a plan of action which can be adapted for different purposes. It can be very reassuring if you have a routine you can depend on to get you started. In addition, the questions to ask yourself, which are listed in the left-hand column above, can be very useful in a number of situations.

Your plan of action to start the work may look something like this:

1. Read through the whole assignment or essay question.

2. Underline any word or phrase I do not understand.

3. Look up those words in the dictionary and choose the most likely meaning in the context. Make a list of their meanings so that I can refer to it while I am working.

4. Ask someone who is helpful to explain any word or phrase that I still do not understand.

5. Use the self-questioning technique on pages 53–56 to make a written plan.

6. If I find it helpful, use a flow diagram or some other type of diagram.

Assignment Plan

What? . . . . .information or materials needed?

Where? . . . . .can the information be found?
                            lecture notes?
                            text book?
                            handouts?
                            library?
                            computer?
                            internet?
                            specialist association?
                            telephone enquiry?
                            somewhere else?

Where to do it? . . . . .college?
                            library?
                            at home?
                            in a specially equipped workshop?
                            in a Field Study Centre?
                            somewhere else?

How to present it? . . . . .written work?
                            diagrams?
                            flow charts?
                            original artwork?
                            clipart?
                            photographs?
                            internet extract?
                            or a combination of some of the above?

When? . . . . .date it is to be completed.

Time Plan

The daily time plan will include:

- ‣ Divide the work into separate sections or tasks.

- ‣ Plan a day, noting how long you expect it to take you to do each section or task.

- ‣ Look at your plan each day. If you do not manage to keep exactly to your time plan modify it and list your reasons for not managing to keep to your original time plan. This will help you to evaluate your progress at the end of the assignment. Very few people manage to be exactly right when they plan their time, but this skill can be acquired by reviewing what you have done at the end. Often it is circumstances beyond your control that may cause you to need a longer or shorter time than you anticipated.

Plan-do-review

When attempting any assignment whether it is an essay, report or practical activity a useful strategy to use is the Plan-do-review sequence.

This sequence can be used by individuals but is also particularly effective when the planning and reviewing. Parts of the sequence can initially be done verbally in small groups. This is very advantageous for people with Asperger's Syndrome because it provides practice in stating a sequence orally. This also provides an opportunity for other members of the group to listen carefully and then give helpful suggestions.

Useful questions to ask at Planning Time

- ‣ I wonder how long my plan will take?
- ‣ What will I do first?
- ‣ Will that take a little while or a long time?
- ‣ If it takes longer than I think, when will I be able to continue with it?
- ‣ What will I do next?
- ‣ How long do I think that will take?

Useful questions to ask at Review Time

- ‣ Did my plan take as long as I estimated?
- ‣ What did I do first?

- ▸ What were the difficulties I encountered?
- ▸ How did I overcome them?
- ▸ How could I have improved my plan?

Review Time for an individual is a chance to evaluate what they have done and provides pointers for improving their skills next time. If review is undertaken in a group situation this gives an opportunity for other students to appreciate the work done. It is also a time where suggestions for alternative ways of overcoming problems can be discussed in a positive manner. This can be an important step towards the gradual introduction of further co-operative work.

Progression in planning

What?	Making simple choices.
Which way?	Identifying alternative courses of action.
Which order?	Considering different sequences of actions.
Possible outcomes?	Anticipating the results of different actions.
Why?	Defining reasons for decisions made.

The above sequences illustrate logical progression in the development of a skill in making decisions. It may take a long time to move through this progression but it is important to have patience in order to preserve confidence.

You may wish to produce your own progression for the development of decision-making skills if it will aid progress.

Activity

Planning assignments and essays.

1. You will need:

   one person with whom you feel comfortable (or a small group) so that you can share ideas

   paper and pen for each person to make notes of the points you want to remember

   the two lists, Independent learning and Assignment, on pages 52–54.

2. Question to think about or discuss:

   Which is the best way for me to plan an assignment or an essay?

3. Action for the group to take:

   Alter the planning sheet to suit your own way of working.

   Discuss the different plans each person has written.

Study skills

Note taking during a lesson or lecture

Many people try to write down everything a teacher or lecturer says during a lesson. This is not efficient because we cannot write as fast as people speak. Also it is not possible to learn everything a teacher says and to remember it in detail. We need some way of helping us to remember the most relevant and important parts of the lesson.

If the teacher or lecturer uses handouts it may not be necessary to take any notes. Handouts are frequently a summary of the main points. If the teacher uses flip charts or overhead transparencies or writes lists or draws diagrams on a blackboard, whiteboard or flip-chart, it may be possible to copy these quickly. Our aim should be to have a summary of important points from the lesson. This gets easier the more you do it. It is a valuable skill, which can aid learning, so it is worth practising.

Some people develop this skill by making a diagram or 'mind-map' of their own which helps them to remember the most important facts or ideas. (Tipper 2002, referring to the Buzan Organisation.)

How to mind-map a holiday

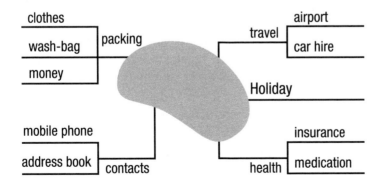

You may find that because teachers and lecturers have different teaching styles, you are able to use different ways of taking notes for each one. It can also be helpful to use a different style of note taking for different subjects. For example, for a lesson on interior design for rooms in a cottage quick diagrams may be appropriate, but for remembering the people in a novel or play a simple list of characteristics may be all that is needed.

Sometimes it is helpful to:

- put the items in alphabetical order
- sequence the items in the order they occur (as in a science experiment)
- sequence the items in the order they are used (as in a recipe for a cake).

It is important to recognise the purpose of the notes you are going to take. Think about how you are going to use them. For most people note taking is an aid to remembering important facts. Students in school need them as an *aide-memoiré* for passing exams. Students at university will also need to pass exams, but in addition they may need their notes to refer to when they take up their work as practising professionals such as doctors, teachers or lawyers.

The main purposes for note making are to:

- write down the most important points to provide information for future reference
- pass exams
- provide starting points for further research.

Note taking is not just useful in lessons or lectures but can also be used when gathering information from different sources. When writing an essay it may be necessary to look in different places (see page 54) and to gather facts and opinions from different sources.

As soon as possible after a lesson, use your handouts or notes to construct a diagram, flow chart or mind-map. It may be helpful to underline the words and phrases that seem to be the most important, and to use these to construct the diagram. When the diagram is finished look at it until you think you know it, then cover it and see how much you can reproduce on another piece of paper. Compare the two diagrams. Notice if you have omitted anything on the second one. In some cases it might help to count the number of items on each diagram. Later in the day, or on the next day, see if you can reproduce the diagram again without missing anything. Do the same thing again after one week. At the end of one month do it again.

In this way you will learn and remember the details you need and your summary diagrams will make it easy to refresh your memory whenever necessary, for example just before an exam. This can save spending a lot of time on revision.

Other useful tips

- ▸ If you have a good sense of humour you could make it a part of your diagram and this may make it easier to remember.

- ▸ Some people think of ways to link each item to the next one, which provides them with a sort of 'memory chain'.

- ▸ Other people use colour to emphasise certain words or phrases. Highlighter pens are useful for this.

- ▸ It may also be helpful to arrange a set of points as though they are the hours on a clock or like a train pulling a line of carriages. See how many different ways you can think of and choose the most appropriate for each particular task.

Developing control

Most adults are in a position of power and control over children and young people. Society expects parents to be able to control their children and this can be extremely difficult for parents whose children have Asperger's Syndrome. Most parents aim to develop self-control in their children, but this is much easier said than done.

In order to develop self-control, children have to learn how to use power appropriately and this means making the right decisions. Self-control and the ability to make appropriate decisions are necessary before independent learning can be developed. Adults often assume that children are unable to make decisions and consequently never give them the opportunity to develop this skill.

In addition, the idea of making their own decisions and taking control of certain situations can be very frightening to some young people and this can make it very difficult for parents or carers to withdraw from the role of organiser and decision maker. For most young people with Asperger's Syndrome it will take longer for them to reach the point where they can lead independent lives but this can often be accomplished with patience and minimal support. In striving to attain independent living, care must be taken to ensure that they are not left in situations where they may be vulnerable.

The Plan-do-review sequence (see page 60) is a means whereby young people can be given the opportunity to make decisions about their activities (either work or leisure) and as they become more experienced they are able to assume control for longer periods of time. This does not mean that parents abdicate from their position of responsibility but that they preserve a balance between what the young person wants to do and what they need to do. On many occasions what they want to do is what they need to do and this is when the quality of motivation, co-operation and learning is at its best. When wants and needs are not the same, tensions may develop, and in such circumstances the Plan-do-review sequence can provide a structure and a calm climate within which it is possible to discuss how difficulties can be overcome without the stress and strain of intense argument.

Developing a concept of time

Many people with Asperger's Syndrome have a poorly developed concept of time. This creates difficulties such as being late for appointments and not managing to complete activities because of lack of time. There are key experiences which we all need to support learning and development in the concept of time. The following experiences will help if they are practised regularly and consistently.

- ‣ Starting and stopping an action on signal.
- ‣ Planning and completing what one has planned.
- ‣ Describing and representing past events (by writing, drawing, photographs and so on).
- ‣ Talking about future events and making appropriate preparations.
- ‣ Noticing, describing and representing the order of events.
- ‣ Experiencing and describing different rates of movement.
- ‣ Using conventional time units when talking about past and future events (such as morning, yesterday, hour).
- ‣ Comparing time periods (short, long; new, old; young, old; a little while, a long time).
- ‣ Observing that clocks and calendars are used to mark the passage of time and using these to plan the daily, weekly and monthly programme.
- ‣ Observing seasonal changes and using this knowledge to plan activities such as holidays and work in the garden.
- ‣ Comparing speeds and duration of events.

- Comparing two different but simultaneous activities.

- Recognising equal durations, despite differences in speed or in starting/stopping points.

- Recalling and predicting a series of events.

- Identifying and representing simultaneous series of events, despite differences in speed or activity.

- Using clocks, timers and calendars to observe the passage of time, to measure time and to anticipate events.

(Adapted from *Young Children in Action* [1979]. Part two: Key experiences for cognitive development.)

It has been found helpful for young children to learn the pattern of their daily routine so that they can foretell what will happen next. This helps them to accept the transition from one activity to another. It is also helpful for them to learn to plan an activity so that they know what they are going to do and what materials or things they need in order to do it. When they have carried out their planned activity it is good for them to review it by telling others what they did and how they did it. This reinforces their learning and helps them to improve future plans. It is a great way to build confidence and independence. Initially, plans may be completed (or abandoned) within a few minutes but eventually children will plan for longer periods of time. It is important to value what they have done, and for them to understand that much can be learned from reviewing abandoned plans. They may find ways to make the plan successful if at sometime they try it again.

Many teenagers, whether they have Asperger's Syndrome or not, may not have developed the ability to plan and so they benefit a lot from activities which help them to develop this skill.

Planning a journey by bus	
Questions to ask	**Actions to take**
What written material do I need?	Obtain the right bus timetable.
Where do I want to go?	
Which buses go there?	
When do I want to arrive?	
How long will it take?	
Can I work out which bus will get me there in time?	Work out the time of departure of the bus that arrives in time.
How long does it take me to walk to the bus stop?	Allow plenty of time to arrive at the bus stop before the bus comes.

Planning the return journey is just as important.

Section 4 Relationships

For most of us the first relationship we form is with our parents and this is often the most lasting relationship we have throughout life. As we grow up we get to know other family members and the friends of our parents. Because we spend a lot of time with our family the relationships within the family usually become very strong. Because our parents also like to spend time with their friends, they quite often become our friends and their children may become our friends too.

When young children start school they get to know the other children in their class. They may particularly like one or two children and so they may spend more time playing with them. Young children change their friends quite often, probably because they need to get to know a lot of children before they can decide which ones they would like to be their special friends. When children reach junior school their friendships become more lasting. It usually takes a long time for a strong friendship to form. It can take months or even years.

By the time children reach the secondary stage of education they usually have friends of the same sex, mainly because they have similar interests. However, there are lots of things which interest both sexes, for example computers, pop groups, films and games. Best friends usually have many interests in common. They play games together and like to talk about their favourite activities and people.

During our lifetime we will probably meet thousands of people. Most of them will be people we only meet once or twice, such as people we meet on holiday, on the bus or at the supermarket checkout. Some of them will become our friends and one or two may become our best friends. Perhaps one very special person will become our partner.

We can think of relationships as a double continuum such as this:

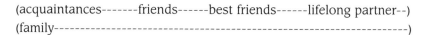

(acquaintances-------friends------best friends------lifelong partner--)
(family--)

Although acquaintances, friends and best friends may change at different times in our lives, usually our family remains constant and lifelong partners may become part of the family.

Friends and acquaintances

Acquaintances are people I know by sight. They can be girls or boys or men or women.

I know that they may:

- go to the same college as I do
- work at the same place as I do
- work in a shop that I go to
- work in a club that I go to
- get the same bus every day that I do
- have been introduced to me by somebody I know well.

Usually I do not know very much about acquaintances and I do not tell them any details about myself or my family. When I meet them I usually smile and say, "Hello!" If I get to know them really well they may become one of my friends.

Friends are people I know well. They can be girls or boys or men or women. I usually know a lot about them.

I may know:

- what they like to do
- what kinds of clothes they like
- who their favourite pop groups are
- what they like to eat.

Usually I see them often:

- I arrange to see them during my leisure time.
- I enjoy their company.
- We may have the same interests.
- We like to do things together.
- They are people who seek me out, for example they often telephone me for a chat, to arrange to go out together or to invite me to a party.
- They may invite me to their house.
- They usually smile when we meet because they are pleased to see me.

Alex often had difficulty in knowing which people were her friends. She thought that everyone she knew were her friends even if they were not very kind to her. Most people, when meeting someone for the first time, automatically observe him or her and listen very carefully to what they say. In this way they try to form an opinion about what their new acquaintance is like. They watch the expressions on their face and look into their eyes to see when they are being serious and when they are joking. Sometimes this is called people watching or mind reading. It is really like a guessing game. It is not easy and it takes a long time to reach a careful opinion about each person we meet.

When people are forming these opinions they often wonder about things like:

- Does he/she look pleased to meet me?
- Does he/she really think that?
- Do his/her actions match the things they say?
- If I was having difficulty would they offer to help me?
- Are most of his/her opinions similar to mine?
- Do we have lots of interests in common?
- Do I like the sound of their voice?
- Do I enjoy their company?

We cannot usually find answers to such questions at a first meeting. It can take many weeks or months to form an opinion about people we meet and whether they have become a real friend. Sometimes we think that someone is a friend and then they do something that makes us change our mind.

Sometimes when they first meet someone people judge others by their appearance. Some time later they may find that their first impression was not the correct one. We cannot always judge people by their appearance. However, we have to remember that if we are going for a job interview or an interview for college, our appearance is important because we have very little time to make a good impression. We need to make sure that our appearance will influence the interviewers in our favour so we try to wear things that are appropriate for work.

Activity

To decide which people you know are friends and which are acquaintances.

1. You will need:

   one person with whom you feel comfortable (or a small group) so that you can share ideas

   paper, pen and scissors for each person to make name labels

   the information on the previous two pages.

2. What to do:

   Write a list of lots of people you know. You may not know all of their names but you may be able to describe them, for example 'the postman' or 'the doctor's receptionist'.

   Cut up the list so that you have each name or description on a small piece of paper.

   Sort the names into two groups labelled 'friends' and 'acquaintances'.

   Tell the person with whom you are working your reasons for including each name in that particular group.

Dating

All people need time to get to know each other. When you are dating someone, you need to get to know them as a friend and feel they are someone you can trust.

What does it mean to trust someone?

It means that you know for sure that it is safe to be alone with them and that they will look after you and never do anything that will hurt you. Until you know someone well and have been in lots of different places with them, watched their behaviour towards you, and thought about how they behave, it is not wise to really trust them.

Never go away for the night with a person who you do not know really well.

To decide whether you can trust someone, you need to think about their behaviour.

With a friend, or in a group, look at the following list and discuss whether you can trust a person who does each of these things.

1. You arrange to meet a friend at a bus stop to go for a drink.

    You get there on time and wait for a long time but the friend doesn't arrive, so you go home.

    The following day your friend telephones to say sorry he/she didn't come and wants to meet you again. What do you say?

2. You go to a disco with a friend and he/she leaves you alone a lot of the time and goes off with other friends. He/she gets drunk and shouts at you.

    The following week he/she telephones you to say that he/she wants to see you again. What do you say?

3. You want to see a friend again but he/she lives in another town. He wants you to travel to see him/her all the time. Sometimes there is no bus and the taxi costs £12.00 for the trip, which you have to pay. Should you continue the relationship?

Romantic relationships

It is natural for young people to want to form a romantic relationship. It may seem to be the fashionable thing to do. It is easy to be attracted towards someone because of their looks and this is often the starting point of a relationship. However, it is very important to get to know them really well before making a serious commitment. The relationship needs to progress slowly at first so that you can get to know them as a real friend without the complication of a close sexual partnership. You may be lucky enough to meet the right person quickly, but at first it is very difficult to guess the real intentions of someone who wants to go out with you. They may only want you for company on one or two occasions or want to appear friendly towards you so that you will satisfy their sexual needs.

Romantic relationships may last only a short time or they may lead to a more permanent relationship such as marriage. It is important to think through carefully your own moral opinions. Think about the following questions.

1. What kind of person do I want for a lifetime partner?

2. Do I think it is wise to get to know somebody really well before we have sex or set up house together?

3. Some diseases are caught through sexual relationships, for example, AIDS, chlamydia, genital herpes. Should I discuss the importance of practising safe sex (using a condom) with a friend who might become a sexual partner?

4. How can I keep myself safe?
   Can I believe what he/she tells me?

5. Do we both understand what living together really means? Can we plan sensibly for somewhere to live and how we will manage our budget?

6. What are our views on contraception and family planning?
   Do we have the same opinions about this?

Activity

Thinking carefully about romantic relationships and trying to form some opinions about them.

1. You will need:

   one person with whom you feel comfortable (or a small group) so that you can share ideas

   paper and pen for each person to make notes of the points they want to remember

   the list of questions above.

2. What to do:

   This is a list of very personal questions. With the person or group with whom you are working, decide which questions you wish to consider.

   Add to the list any other questions you think it is important to discuss. If you are part of a discussion group consider carefully everyone's opinions and ideas.

Valuing people

It is sometimes difficult to form an opinion about people and it can be helpful to think about the qualities you value. Ask yourself the following questions about your present boy or girl friend.

Which of these things does he/she do?

- Tells you that you are important to him/her.

- Listens to what you have to say.

- He/she doesn't let anybody annoy you while he/she is around.

- Wants to see you regularly but not every day, so that you both have different things to tell each other about when you meet.

- Wants to know about you, for example, knows your favourite colour, book, flower, singer.

- Takes you places he/she knows you like, even if it's only a walk along the road.

- Sometimes brings you some of your favourite food.

- Remembers little things that you like, for example, an actor's photograph, a piece of music and wants to share them with you.

- Plans things together with you.

- When he/she makes a promise, they always keep it.

- Tries to share in one or two of your favourite activities, for example, card games or swimming.

- Sometimes takes you to a special event.

- Gives you useful information that he/she knows you need.

- Remembers things that upset you and tries to keep them away from you.

- You know that you can believe what he/she says.

Which of these things does he/she do?

- Tries to get you to do things that he/she knows your family do not want you to do.

- Asks you to share secrets with him/her and not tell your family.

- Makes plans for your future with him/her without discussing it with your family.

- Thinks about his/her own needs and how he/she needs your company, but doesn't think about your needs and whether he/she can help you with them.

- Lets you down by not arriving on time.

- Does not give you equal importance with him/herself.
- Gives you extra problems of his/her own but doesn't help you with your problems.
- Asks you to try some drugs.
- Gets drunk, telephones you and shouts at you down the phone.
- Makes his/her own decisions about what you will both do, and then tells you to do them.
- Says he/she hasn't got any money and wants to share yours.
- Tells you things that you later discover are not true.
- Leaves you on your own when you don't want to be alone.
- Wants you to stay with him/her overnight in the house of some people you do not know.

Intimate relationships

People with Asperger's Syndrome have difficulty understanding the thoughts and feelings of others and this can cause misunderstandings and embarrassment. As a result they often prefer to talk about issues concerning sex, masturbation and menstruation with their peers or brothers and sisters if they have them.

Questions that might arise include:

How does it feel to be with another person?

What is the difference between a close friend and a boyfriend or girlfriend?

What are the methods of contraception and the consequences of not using contraception?

How do you say 'no' to somebody without upsetting them?

How do you tell when somebody is taking you for granted?

How do you negotiate or compromise with your boyfriend or girlfriend?

How do you avoid dangerous situations?

For girls:

What is premenstrual tension (PMT) and what can be done about it?

What are the methods of sanitary protection?

How and when do you use it (for example, if you go swimming you must use a tampon)?

How do you dispose of soiled sanitary protection?

When and where to talk about it and with whom – how to be discreet.

These topics may well have been discussed during sex education classes in school but it may be helpful for young people with Asperger's Syndrome to discuss them again in small groups.

Allocating time to maintain friendships

Most people value their friends because they are reliable and loyal. If a friend lets you down it causes disappointment and perhaps some trouble in order to change the arrangements.

It is most important to use a calendar on the wall to write down, on each day of the week, where you are going with your friends and at what time. This will avoid double-booking anything. After all, you can't be in two different places at the same time!

Playing a card game in a group

Card games such as whist, bridge or magic are played in groups of four with two partners working together against the opposing team. If one person drops out, then it is impossible for the others to play this kind of 4-player game and so they have to change the kind of game they play so that they work as individuals instead of partners. They may even have to cancel their arrangements altogether.

Alex's group of four can only meet on a day and at a time when they are not working. This means that some members of the group may have to change some of their plans so that they are available when the others are free. Once a day of the week has been chosen when all of them can be there they should all stick to that day and time, because the group depends on all of the members being there at the same time. They all need each other. When a group agrees to meet at the same time every week this is called making a commitment. This is a plan to give time regularly. It is not something that any member of the group should change at a moment's notice. The rest of their activities should be arranged at other times on other days so that the arranged time is kept free for the group. If you make a similar arrangement to do a particular activity with a group, mark on the calendar every week that this is the time your group meets. Mark lots of weeks at one time – write it in every week for two or three months.

It is not easy to find another group of people with the same interests, so give it value in your thinking. Think to yourself, "I am not going to give up that time unless it is for something really important." (Really important things might be appointments with doctors, specialists or your college tutors.)

Let us say that you agree to meet your card group on Thursday afternoons. One day, a friend from college rings you up and invites you to go somewhere with them on Thursday. What do you say? Instead of saying, "Yes" straight away, look at your calendar. Remember that you will be letting down your group if you say you are free then. There are many possible Thursdays when your group can meet, but this invitation is for one day only. The membership of the group is more important than a single trip out with another person and the rest of your group will be disappointed if they have to change their arrangements. But what do you say to the friend on the phone? You don't want to miss an opportunity to go out with another friend. You could try to arrange a different day of the week or ask if you can talk to them in college about a time when you are both free. Instead of saying, "No, I can't go" you could say, "That's the day I meet my card group. Could I meet you on a different day?" It may be that other times to meet this friend can be arranged in the future.

Making a regular commitment to do something you enjoy

Let us suppose that your aunt invites you to go swimming on Monday afternoons. You really enjoy swimming but you keep forgetting to talk to her about times to meet up with each other. Your aunt sometimes forgets too, but she needs regular exercise so it would be very helpful to her if you reminded her instead of waiting for her to remind you. When you don't telephone her to make arrangements, she may think that you can't be bothered. How can you make sure that you go swimming regularly with her? It is important to set aside some time to think about it and maybe talk to someone about it.

1) Contact her each week to arrange a time to meet (or tell her if you can't go).

2) Before the meeting time, collect together everything you will need for swimming. Make a checklist so that you do not forget anything.

Don't forget to look at the weather on the day that you are swimming and collect together suitable shoes and coat if it is raining, gloves and a scarf if it is cold. Don't leave this until your aunt arrives.

Remember that it is your responsibility to put your gloves in a safe place, not anyone else's. Get into the habit of always putting them in a special place when you take them off, such as in your coat pockets, so that you can always find them again the next time you need them.

You must realise that your aunt has already spent time collecting her things together in time to meet you as arranged.

At the same time that she is getting her things ready at her house, you should be getting your things ready at your house.

Your aunt does not want to spend time getting things ready at her house and then have to waste time waiting while you get your things ready. This is what it means when two people arrange to meet at a particular time. They are promising each other that they will get themselves ready properly beforehand so that they can enjoy being together at that special time with no hassle.

If one person is never ready on time, they are wasting the other person's time. It makes the other person think that they are not prepared to do the work of getting themselves ready, so maybe they don't value the friendship because they are not prepared to put any effort into it.

People know that they must keep some time available before any meeting, to get their things ready, so that neither of them has to wait for the other one.

It may be a good idea to pack the swimming bag the day before, and get the outdoor clothes ready on the day of the trip to the swimming pool.

When you mark on your calendar what time you will meet, it may be a good idea to mark on the calendar when to get your things ready so that you are sure to be ready on time.

Do not make another appointment in the hour before you go out, because that would take away the time that you need to get yourself ready.

If you know what time you expect to be back, this would be useful information in case someone is planning to make a meal for you, or if they were planning to go out themselves.

Your calendar might look like this:

MONDAY

3.30 get clothes and bag ready for swimming.
4.30 leave for swimming
Back home at 6.30 approximately

Use the calendar for monthly, weekly and daily plans and to remind you of anything that you might forget. Write in the things that happen lots of times and things that only happen once.

When you have made the final arrangements, mark off all of the Mondays for the next three months so that you can see when you will be swimming. You will be able to see a pattern of going swimming on Mondays. You will see other patterns of things that you do every week like going to college or your club.

Look at your calendar every day and plan the day ahead and the week ahead. Your calendar keeps you in touch with your plans for each day and each week.

Copy information from your diary onto your calendar. For example if you make appointments when you are not at home write them in your diary and then when you get home copy them onto your calendar. If you don't do this you may forget to turn up for your appointments.

> When your diary is closed, you can't see inside it, but when the calendar is hanging on the wall and you walk past it lots of times during the day, it is a good reminder for you.

Try to be ready when your friends arrive. They have come to spend some enjoyable time with you and if you are not ready you are spoiling their enjoyment of your time together.

Making arrangements by telephone

A good place to keep your calendar is hanging on the wall beside the telephone. If anyone phones to make a date with you it is easy to refer to the arrangements you have already made.

> When someone telephones you to make arrangements to meet you, don't agree to any day or time until you have checked on the calendar whether you are free.

If your calendar is not by the telephone tell them that you have to check your diary and you will ring them back in five minutes. (Make sure that you have their telephone number before they ring off, otherwise you won't be able to ring them back!)

Arguments

Many people with Asperger's Syndrome find it difficult to discuss things without the discussion developing into an argument. This usually happens because they are nervous about the topic being discussed or because they are being persuaded to do something that does not appeal to them. When a discussion between two people becomes very heated, other people who may be nearby are tempted to join in. This can result in the person with Asperger's Syndrome feeling that everybody is against them and so they stick rigidly to their opinion and nothing will persuade them to change their mind. The people who are trying to influence them may begin to feel that they are being unreasonable and so the argument escalates. It is not helpful to argue with someone with Asperger's Syndrome.

It can be very difficult to keep in mind all the reasons given during a discussion and whenever Alex appears to be quite stubborn in her opinions it has been helpful to write down all the pros and cons. She can then read them and take some time to consider the different reasons for alternative courses of action.

For example, at her training establishment it was suggested to her that she should consider doing some work experience as a way into finding the right job. Three people tried to persuade her that this would be beneficial. This alarmed her and caused her to immediately reject the suggestion. When she arrived home she was obviously agitated about it. We sat down and made a list of all the reasons why she did not think that it was a good idea. Then we listed all the reasons why it might possibly be a really good idea. This calmed her down and gave her some time to think about the situation.

Work experience

Alex's difficulties	Positive aspects
If she were not appointed to a permanent job it would seem pointless.	Work experience is a type of training on the job.
She would get used to the job and then might have to leave.	If not appointed it might save her being a 'square peg in a round hole' having to do a job she doesn't like.
She may be paid less than the job is worth and so she would not be motivated.	It is a chance to learn gradually and to demonstrate how good she is.
She might have to wait a long time before a decision is reached about a permanent post.	The time would not be wasted as it gives her an opportunity to try different jobs and gain a greater variety of experience.
The hours may be difficult and may not fit in with her training days.	The hours would be negotiated to fit in with other training if necessary.
Unsure of how it works and how it would be beneficial.	Opportunity to try out different jobs, to work with different people and to learn about different organisations.
Who to turn to if there are confrontations.	Sometimes write it down like this, itemising difficulties and positive aspects, and sometimes consult with your support worker.

Independence

Being independent means not depending on another person for one's opinion or livelihood. It means being self-reliant, self- sufficient, self-assured, on one's own and by oneself. Everyone can be independent to some degree and it is a characteristic that usually develops gradually throughout life.

A baby is totally dependent on its parents until it becomes independently mobile when it can crawl or walk. Once this happens it can move towards objects it wants to explore so that it can play with them. Young children achieve more independence when their parents know that they can safely leave them to play in another room without supervision, and this independence is further increased when they are allowed to play outside in the garden. At the same time children become able to take care of their own needs such as going to the toilet when necessary and being able to take a shower and dress themselves. Different children achieve these skills at different ages. The amount of independence which parents allow their children is based on how much responsibility the children are able to take for their own behaviour and the safety of the child is usually the most important factor to be considered.

When children become teenagers they begin to want to make their own decisions and this often causes conflict if their parents feel that they will not make the best decisions for their future. For example, parents do not like their teenagers to stay out late at night because it may put them in danger and also if they do not get enough sleep they will upset their body-clock and endanger their health. In turn this will make them tired the next day and their studies may suffer with the result that their whole future career may be put at risk. For teenagers it is often difficult to take the long term view, especially if their friends do not care about their studies. It can be very difficult if one is not conforming to group values and opinions. This can be a great test of one's ability to be sensibly independent and take the right course for one's future happiness.

The greatest degree of independence is usually achieved when young people set up their own home. For many this is not complete independence because they share their accommodation with a friend or with fellow students at college or university. They are partially dependent on whoever they share with because they will need their financial contribution for the rent and fuel and so on. People only become totally independent when they are living alone and are responsible for all their own material and emotional needs.

Many people are so gregarious that they would not like to live alone, but for other people this is the ideal situation. When people get married or decide to live together they become mutually dependent on each other. If they decide to have a family this has to be a joint decision because they are taking on responsibility for other human beings who will be totally dependent on them for many years to come. Many people have the mistaken idea that with independence comes freedom. This is not usually the case because with freedom comes responsibility. To begin with it may only be responsibility for one's own safety and well-being but if one lives with someone else it involves taking on a certain amount of responsibility for them. If one has a family this involves a huge amount of responsibility because babies are very demanding and have to be cared for 24 hours a day. It is a commitment for a large part of your life and in some cases maybe for the rest of your life. In addition the parent or carer has to provide enough money to run the home as well as looking after the children. It costs a great deal of money to bring up a child so it is important to plan ahead and to realise that the way you decide your future career is vital not just for your own happiness but for the happiness of your whole family, both present and future.

For people with Asperger's Syndrome there is an additional aspect to consider. Before a couple start a family it may be advisable for them to have genetic counselling. If there appears to be a genetic factor in their Asperger's Syndrome they may decide that the best option for them would be to consider adopting one or two children if they are sufficiently financially and emotionally independent to provide a good home for them.

Conclusion

Alex's view

I feel I can manage in social situations a lot better than when I was first diagnosed in 1996, due to my maturity and careful guidance from my Gran. I enjoy going to my local Asperger's Pub and Youth clubs. I have also enjoyed going abroad on a study visit with my college group.

By the time I was sixteen I managed to get 3Bs, 4Cs and 2Ds in my GCSEs, and Youth Award Scheme silver level. I moved on to Weston College and got various office, accountancy and computing qualifications, before moving to City of Bristol College to study computing and science at A level standard.

In the past I have tried various tablets for depression and found that I reacted badly to many of them. I don't take any now and I feel much better without them.

I feel I can control my Asperger's Syndrome rather than it controlling me and I rarely get upset without being able to control myself.

At present I am attending a course entitled Intimate Relationships. It is a very good course and I am learning a great deal. There should be more courses like this for people with Asperger's Syndrome.

Next September I am hoping to go to Bath Spa University at Newton Park to study Food, Nutrition and Consumer Protection. In the future I hope to become a dietician and if possible work with autistic children and their families.

Gran's view

Alex is a bright girl with a lovely sense of humour. Like many young people she has found the teenage years very difficult. This time of life holds more risks for those with Asperger's Syndrome and their vulnerability means that independence is achieved much later than usual. However, Alex is very caring towards her peers who encounter similar problems and does her best to help them. She has worked hard at her studies and shows determination to succeed. I am sure that she will be able to contribute to society and have a happy, satisfying future.

Bibliography

Attwood, T. (1997), *Asperger's Syndrome: A Guide for Parents and Professionals*. London, Jessica Kingsley Publishers Ltd.

Buzan, T. (1974) *Use your Head*. London, BBC Books.

Collins COBUILD *Dictionary of Idioms* (second edition 2002). London, Harper Collins.

Alex has recently acquired this second edition. The first one was so well used that it fell to bits! She finds it invaluable as it explains all kinds of sayings which most of us take for granted. It makes interesting reading for anyone although it was compiled for people learning English as a foreign language.

Cumine, V., Leach, J. & Stevenson, G. (1998) *Asperger's Syndrome: A practical Guide for Teachers*. London, David Fulton Publishers Ltd.

We found this book particularly helpful. Alex read it and underlined all of the things she thought applied to her. She then asked Maude to underline anything relevant she had missed (see pages 5 to 8). Their resulting document was then discussed with her tutors.

Frith, U. (1991) [Editor] *Autism and Asperger's Syndrome*, Cambridge, Cambridge University Press.

Grandin,T. *My Experiences with Visual Thinking, Sensory Problems and Communication Difficulties*, http//www.autism.org/temple/visual.html

Hohmann,M., Banet,B. & Weikart, D.P. (1979) *Young Children in Action*. Michigan, The High/Scope Press.

Leicester City Council and Leicestershire County Council (1998) *Asperger's Syndrome - practical strategies for the classroom: A teacher's guide*. London, The National Autistic Society.

Although this is another book for staff in school, many of the strategies transfer quite well to the home setting.

Rinaldi, W. (revised 2001) *Social Use of Language Programme* (SULP). Windsor, N.F.E.R. Nelson.

This programme is suitable for use with secondary age and adult students. It may be used with individuals or groups.

Roesch, R. (1998) *Time Management for Busy People*. New York, McGraw Hill.

Alex uses this book a lot. It is good for her to decide what is helpful to her and it helps her to be more independent.

Sainsbury, C. (2000) *Martian in the Playground*. Bristol, Lucky Duck Publishing Ltd.

Tipper, M. (2002) *The Positively Mad Guide to the Secrets of Successful Students*. Bristol, Lucky Duck Publishing Ltd.

Williams, Donna. (1996) *Autism, An Inside-Out Approach*. London, Jessica Kingsley Publishers Ltd.